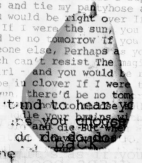

stunt

barenaked ladies

Arranged by John Curtin

Special thanks to Alexandria Stuart, Nettwerk Management

Project Manager: Aaron Stang
Book Art Layout: Jorge Paredes
CD Design/Illustrations: John Rummen at Artwerks Design
Photography: Jay Blakesburg

WARNER BROS. PUBLICATIONS - THE GLOBAL LEADER IN PRINT
USA: 15800 NW 48th Avenue, Miami, FL 33014

WARNER/CHAPPELL MUSIC
CANADA: 40 SHEPPARD AVE. WEST, SUITE 800
TORONTO, ONTARIO, M2N 6K9
SCANDINAVIA: P.O. BOX 533, VENDEVAGEN 85 B
S-182 15, DANDERYD, SWEDEN
AUSTRALIA: P.O. BOX 353
3 TALAVERA ROAD, NORTH RYDE N.S.W. 2113

NUOVA CARISCH
ITALY: VIA CAMPANIA, 12
20098 S. GIULIANO MILANESE (MI)
ZONA INDUSTRIALE SESTO ULTERIANO
SPAIN: MAGALLANES, 25
28015 MADRID
FRANCE: 25 RUE DE HAUTEVILLE, 75010 PARIS

INTERNATIONAL MUSIC PUBLICATIONS LIMITED
ENGLAND: SOUTHEND ROAD,
WOODFORD GREEN, ESSEX IG8 8HN
GERMANY: MARSTALLSTR. 8, D-80539 MUNCHEN
DENMARK: DANMUSIK, VOGNMAGERGADE 7
DK 1120 KOBENHAVNK

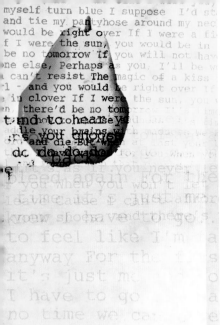

barenaked ladies

CONTENTS

I'LL BE THAT GIRL

Words and Music by
STEPHEN DUFFY and STEVEN PAGE

I'll Be That Girl - 9 - 1
0307B

6

I'll Be That Girl - 9 - 4
0307B

ALCOHOL

Words and Music by
STEPHEN DUFFY and STEVEN PAGE

CALL AND ANSWER

Words and Music by
STEPHEN DUFFY and STEVEN PAGE

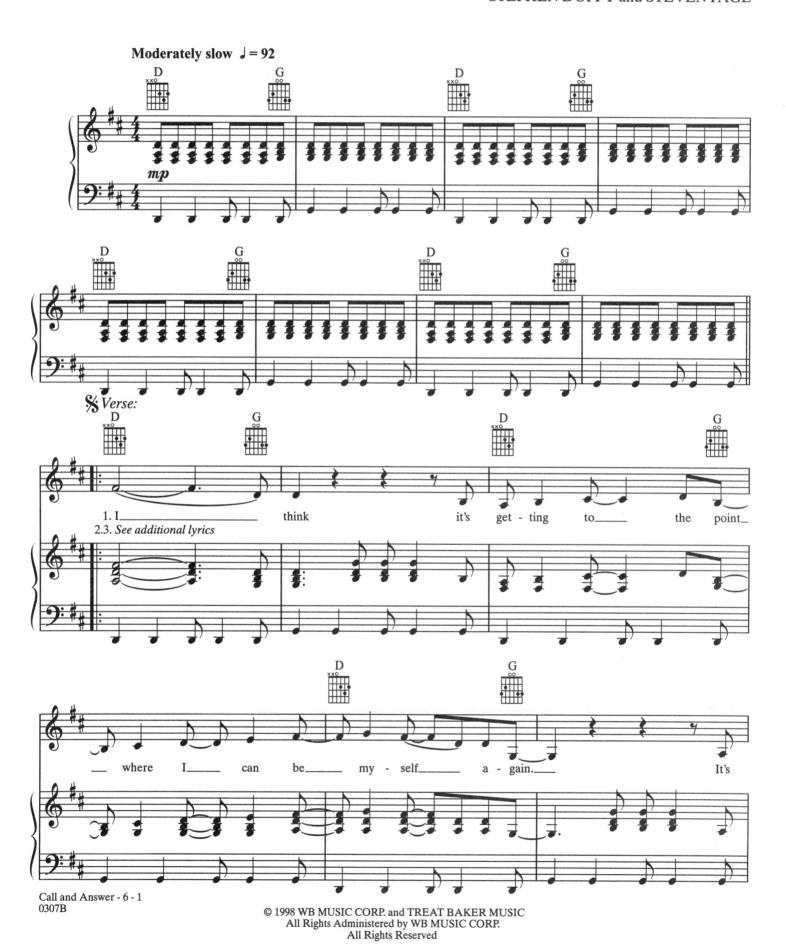

24

Verse 2:
You think I only think about you
When we're both in the same room.
You think I'm only here to witness
The remains of love exhumed.
You think we're here to play
A game of who-loves-more-than-whom.
(To Chorus:)

Verse 3:
You think it's only fair to do what's best for
You and you alone.
You think it's only fair to do the same to me
When you're not home.
I think it's time to make this something that is
More than only fair.
(To Chorus:)

IN THE CAR

Words and Music by
STEVEN PAGE

Moderately fast ♩ = 138

1. She fed me straw-ber-ries_____ and
2.3. *See additional lyrics*

In the Car - 6 - 1
0307B

Verse 2:
A book-and-record love,
We sat and read our books
Between those longing looks,
Compounded by our fear.
My tongue inside her ear,
My tongue inside her,
In the basement of her mother's
House where we once taped the
First three sides of *Sandanista!* for my car.
(To Chorus:)

Verse 3:
Once I had this dream
Where I slept with her mom.
Unless I've got this wrong,
A secret all along.
Unless she hears this song,
Unless she hears it
On a tape inside her car
With her new husband, and she
Turns to him and says, "I think that's me."
(To Chorus 2:)

Chorus 2:
In the car
We were looking for ourselves,
But found each other.
In the car
We groped for excuses
Not to be alone anymore.
In the car
We were waiting for our lives
To start their endings.
In the car
We were never making love,
We were never making love,
We were never making love.

IT'S ALL BEEN DONE

Words and Music by
STEVEN PAGE

It's All Been Done - 5 - 2
0307B

It's All Been Done - 5 - 4
0307B

LIGHT UP MY ROOM

Words by
STEVEN PAGE and ED ROBERTSON

Music by
ED ROBERTSON

1. A hy-dro-

% *Verses 1, 2, & 4:*

field cuts through my neigh-bor-hood; some-how that al-ways just made_ me feel good._
2. 4. *See additional lyrics*

Light Up My Room - 5 - 1
0307B

Verse 2:
Late at night when the wires in the walls
Sing in tune with the din of the falls,
I'm conducting it all while I sleep
To light this whole town.
(To Chorus:)

Verse 4:
There are luxuries we can't afford,
But at our house we never get bored.
We can dance to the radio station
That plays in our teeth.
(To Chorus:)

LEAVE

Words and Music by
STEVEN PAGE and ED ROBERTSON

Moderate rock shuffle ♩ = 72

1. I've in-formed you to leave,
2.3. *See additional lyrics*

'cause I can't af-ford to lose___ more___

To Coda
1.
Em7
A7
C (9)
do, whoa. Do do do do, do
Bm7
D
A7sus
C (9)
G
do do.
D
A7sus
C (9)
G
D
A7sus
C (9)
G
D
A7sus
C (9)
G
2.
do.

Bridge:

when you won't let me for - get?_____

do_____ do do._____

Verse 2:
I've informed you to leave,
'Cause I can't stand to hear you breathe.
I chew up and I choke down
The scraps you choose to leave around.
(To Chorus:)

Verse 3:
I've informed you to leave,
'Cause I can't afford to lose more sleep.
There's your shoes and there's the door.
Please don't come here anymore.
(To Chorus:)

NEVER IS ENOUGH

Words by
STEVEN PAGE and ED ROBERTSON

Music by
ED ROBERTSON

52

get a job at Wen - dy's and are hon - ored with Em - ploy - ee of the

Month.

Chorus:

I think nev-er is e-nough, (yeah, nev-er is e-nough.) I nev-er want to do that stuff.

D D/C# D/B D/A G G/F# Em7 A7
F# F#/E# F#/D# F#/C# B B/A# G#m7 C#7
I think nev-er is e - nough, (yeah, nev-er is e - nough.) You nev-er have to do that stuff.
D D/C# D/B D/A G G/F#
F# F#/E# F#/D# F#/C# B B/A#
I think nev-er is e - nough, (yeah, nev-er is e - nough.) I nev - er want to
Em7 A7 D D/C# D/B D/A
G#m7 C#7 F# F#/E# F#/D# F#/C#
do that stuff. I think nev - er is e - nough, (yeah, nev - er is e -
G G/F# Em7 A7 D
B B/A# G#m7 C#7 F#
nough.) You nev - er have to to that stuff.

SOME FANTASTIC
(Ivory and Ivory)

Words and Music by
STEVEN PAGE and ED ROBERTSON

1. One___ day I_____ will build___ a foun- tain, drink and nev-
2. One___ day I_____ will work___ with an - i -mals; all the tests

Some Fantastic - 10 - 1
0307B

TOLD YOU SO

Words and Music by
STEVEN PAGE and ED ROBERTSON

Verse 2:
I never told you I agreed with you.
I don't think I do.
I wasn't sure quite what the whole thing meant,
But I'm glad you went.
I never thought that it could be painless,
But it is, I guess.
I had myself fooled into needing you.
Did I fool you too?
(To Chorus:)

Verse 3:
I never mentioned how I've prayed for you,
And now I've paid for you.
I never said that I would wait for you.
It's too late for you.
(To Chorus:)

ONE WEEK

Words and Music by
ED ROBERTSON

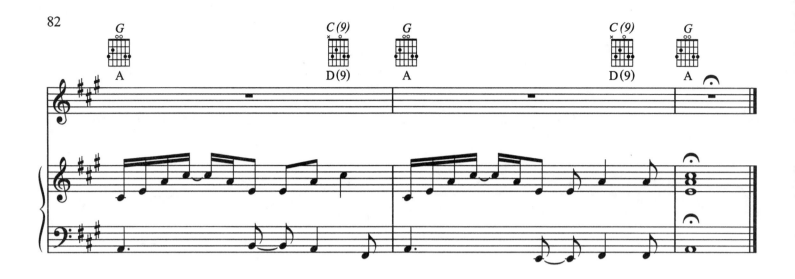

Verse 2:
Chickity China the Chinese chicken,
Have a drumstick and your brain stops tickin'.
Watchin' X-Files with no lights on.
We're dans la maison.
I hope the Smoking Man's in this one.
Like Harrison Ford, I'm getting frantic.
Like Sting, I tantric.
Like Snickers, guaranteed to satisfy.
Like Kurasawa, I make mad films.
OK, I don't make films,
But if I did, they'd have a Samurai.
Gonna get a set a' better clubs;
Gonna find the kind with tiny nubs
Just so my irons aren't always flying
Off the backswing.
Gotta get in tune with Sailor Moon,
'Cause the cartoon has got
The boom Anime babes
That make me think the wrong thing.

Bridge 2:
How can I help it if I think you're funny
When you're mad?
Tryin' hard not to smile though I feel bad.
I'm the kind of guy who laughs at a funeral.
Can't understand what I mean?
You soon will.
I have a tendency to wear
My mind on my sleeve.
I have a history of losing my shirt.

Chorus 3:
It's been one week since you looked at me,
Dropped you arms to your sides
And said, "I'm sorry."
Five days since I laughed at you and said,
"You just did just what I thought
You were gonna do."
Three days since the living room.
We realized we're both to blame,
But what could we do?
Yesterday you just smiled at me
'Cause it'll still be two days
Till we say we're sorry.

WHEN YOU DREAM

Words by
STEVEN PAGE and ED ROBERTSON

Music by
ED ROBERTSON

Moderately slow ♩ = 120

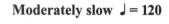

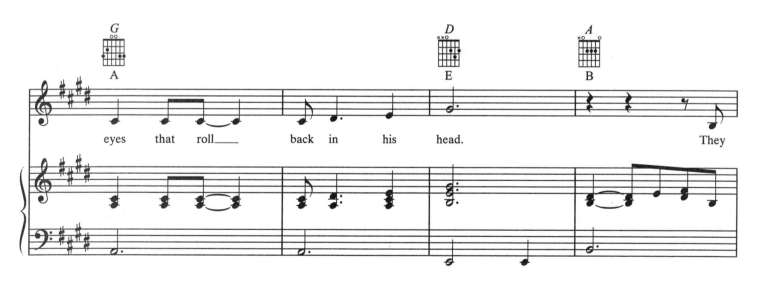

1. With life just be-gun,___ my sleep-ing___ new___ son has

2. See additional lyrics

eyes that roll___ back in his head. They

When You Dream - 7 - 1
0307B

Chorus 3:

an - gels who sing lull - a - bies?____
2. His

3. Do you hear Del Shan - non's___ "Run - a - way"___ play - ing on

tran - sis - tor ra - di - o___ waves? With so

lit - tle ex - pe - ri - ence,___ your mind not yet cog - ni - zant,___ are

Verse 2:
His fontanel pulses with lives that he's lived,
With memories he'll learn to ignore.
And when it is closed, he already knows
He's forgotten all he knew before.
But when sleep sets in,
History begins,
But the future will win.
(To Chorus 2:)

Chorus 2:
When you dream,
What do you dream about?
When you dream,
What do you dream about?
Are they color or black and white,
Yiddish or English,
Or languages not yet conceived?
Are they silent or boisterous?
Do you hear noises just
Loud enough to be perceived?
(To Chorus 3:)

WHO NEEDS SLEEP?

Words and Music by
STEVEN PAGE and ED ROBERTSON